THINGS THAT DISAPPEAR

I

Palace of the Republic

When the Palace of the Republic opened, I was in third grade. My teacher was named Fräulein Kies, and Fräulein Kies held an envelope bearing an image of the new palace up above her head and explained to us what a first day cover was. At the time, it didn't occur to me that the phrase "first day cover" had the same number of syllables, and almost exactly the same vowels, as "nine day wonder." Fräulein Kies said that each of us was going to get one of those first day covers, and that we should take good care of it, because one day we'd be proud that we were there when the new palace opened. After Fräulein Kies presented those first day covers to us, we went on a class field trip to the newly opened palace of the people.

At the time, I still wanted to study archaeology and learn to excavate palaces, so I especially liked the various types of marble that were used downstairs by the coatroom. Upstairs, in the painting gallery, everything was carpeted. Higher up, near the ceiling, there were glass lamps that hung down like air bubbles, so you could imagine you were under water. Those lamps had been provided by the company where my aunt Sigrid worked. The same company provided the utensils for the palace's café—in other words, the spoons that I used in the following years of my life, at first to stir my cocoa, and later my coffee, and the knives and forks in the wine bar that I used to cut into a ham hock or Hawaiian schnitzel when my first boyfriend took me out to eat. It was in the Palace of the Republic that I pinched my finger between two balls while bowling, that I resolved to become a pianist after attending a famous pianist's concert in the theater on the fifth floor, that I dragged the heavy, wrought iron stools in the wine bar overlooking the Spree into position to make myself comfortable.

When it became clear, years later, that the palace was gradually losing its republic, I slipped one of the spoons that my aunt had provided into my pocket for safekeeping. Just three days ago, when I drove past the palace, I could see all the way through it from one side to the other. The demolition started in the middle, perhaps for structural reasons, so the parts with some substance remaining now frame the middle, which is basically made only of air. I thought of Fräulein Kies again, and I wondered if she was calling herself Frau Kies by now, even if no man had ever married her.

II

Bulky Trash

As soon as the owner of an old wardrobe/television/
bicycle pushes it off the ramp, as soon as it's "in there,"
as they say at the Berlin Sanitation Department's waste
disposal sites, it no longer belongs to him; instead, it
becomes the property of the department. The Berlin
Sanitation Department takes possession of the item for
one sole purpose: to remove it from the city and destroy
it appropriately. The moment private owners relinquish
their ownership, the items are henceforth referred to
only by the material they're made of. Wood to wood,
metal to metal, and so on—these are the names the city
uses when it snatches up the old stuff, devours it, along
with any function and use value it might still have,
along with any surplus value and history it might have
had, because only when the old thing has completely

disappeared does a resident of this city, a consumer in the marketplace, buy something new.

If that bike over there hadn't already been labeled "metal," it would certainly still be rideable. *But I tell you, that don't even cross our minds, there'd be a line all the way from here to Kreuzberg*, say the men who lock the containers and cart them away. In the old days, people used to put their old wardrobes out on the street, and they'd always be gone in no more than a night. There were lines due to shortages during the war, and even later in the East, but that's where they're supposed to stay: in history books, in black-and-white photos, in eyewitness accounts. In the West, there were always bananas, and that's how it's supposed to stay. *We're just tryin' to do our job, too*, the men say. *And if we had a bunch of folks crawlin' around here—trash pickers, I call 'em—there wouldn't be any room for the folks who just wanna throw stuff away.* Not even the men themselves are allowed to pick out anything that's "in there." What if, say, you end up with a one of a kind Biedermeier wardrobe? *Nope, not even then.* So if I were to climb into the dumpster (crawl around in the trash), I'd be able to touch an abandoned piece of furniture like that, but in legal terms, it still would have disappeared completely? *Yup.* I wouldn't even be allowed to buy the wardrobe from you? *Nope. Well, I mean, on a personal level you might, human error, you know, that's been known to happen. But it ain't allowed.*

What I don't ask, but would still like to know, is whether the beauty of a wardrobe like that emerges again after it's been chopped to pieces and flies up to heaven, as souls are said to do, and whether the wood itself would be a few grams lighter than before.

People from faraway lands often sit in front of the waste disposal sites, waiting to take televisions, fridges, and speakers before they're thrown away, before they disappear. Unfortunately, I haven't found out yet whether there's even a word for Biedermeier in their languages, and if so, what it is. Now my last hope lies in so-called human error.

III

Memories

The farewells are what I remember. How thin and white R. looked beneath his shock of hair when I said goodbye to him for the last time and he nodded to me without lifting his head from the pillow, just briefly closing his eyes. How I didn't go back to his bed, but simply closed the door behind me. The next day I had to pick up his things from the hospital, including the razor I'd charged for him the day before. The razor was charged, but R. was dead.

When I left my grandmother's house, she was standing at the window of a dark room, waving as I walked away, her silhouette illuminated only by the light that burned behind her in the hallway where we had just said our goodbyes. Two days later she fell, and when I saw her again, her face motionless and her eyes closed, she was lying in a coma in the hospital, where some time later she died.

I remember how R. would nod after he had examined something—a car, a new apartment—I remember how he would hum along under his breath when there was gypsy music playing in a Hungarian restaurant, I remember how he would hunch his shoulders when he was carrying a tray back to the kitchen. I still recall how my grandmother used to say "Oh dear, oh dear" when she was in a hurry and didn't know what to do first, I remember her hands with their gnarled fingernails and her laughter. I already find it hard to recall whether her mouth was open or closed when she laughed, but at least I know how it sounded, and how her laughter gradually faded into laughter at herself.

There's very little that I can touch, see, and hear with my memory anymore. The thoughts of someone who no longer exists can be translated into my thoughts, and the actions of that person into my actions, but the tangible part of those memories will probably fall to pieces sooner or later. When reality no longer grows back, it will become a skeleton, individual bones with a great deal of soil in between. Recently, it's often happened that I find myself sitting across from someone who's still perfectly alive, yet looking at him as if he had already disappeared. At those moments, half hopeful, half ashamed, I pick out single frames of the film while it's still running, as if I could select my memories in advance and learn them by heart, so that I could be sure to recall them later. As for myself, I've already considered whether anyone will remember the way I blow my nose, or the way I watch a boxing match on TV, or my knees.

IV

Nursery School

It all started when the nursery school that my son had been attending sold off one half of its yard, so the fence was moved back closer to the school building. After the jungle gym was relocated, chunks of concrete from its base were left lying in the abandoned sandbox, a waste-basket quickly filled up with dirt and trash because no one was emptying it anymore, and recently a mother found a couple of rather enormous teeth in there. She was standing there with the teeth in her hand when I came to pick up my son, and she asked me if she ought to go to the police now and report it. I looked at the teeth and they looked too big to have come from a person, or even from a dog. It seemed possible to me that, as the site was growing wild, deeper layers had come to the surface and found their way to the trash, so the teeth might have belonged to a cow, or to a giant, antediluvian lizard.

The next message that we parents received concerned the decision made by the responsible authorities to close the nursery school down entirely. True, the sinks are wobbly, the coatrack where my son hangs his jacket looks just as faded as the one where I hung my own red vinyl coat when I still wore a child's size 4—the coat hooks are still attached to those little plastic pictures of animals and fruits that used to be produced in Zschopau—and the boiler room has flooded twice. The building would have to be gutted and fully renovated, they said, and it would cost at least half a million euros. As we nod, we imagine in our minds' eyes all of the things that make it necessary to demolish what's already here because they'd just be too expensive: sinks made of lapis lazuli, mahogany flooring, forty black and forty white slaves and an equal number of eunuchs to serve the children, and play sand delivered fresh each morning from the Gobi Desert. Of course, utopias sometimes cause the disappearance of what was there before, but in this unusual case it is the impracticability of a utopia that makes the demolition necessary. We parents hear the school's prime location in the Mitte district of

Berlin described as a helicopter landing pad, and it isn't entirely clear whether this is meant as a joke, a technical term, or a real federal government building project.

As he bids farewell to his old nursery school, my son gives his favorite tree—a thoroughly mediocre pine tree—a goodbye kiss on its rough bark. We've already been informed that this pine tree, as well as an apple tree and a few bushes, will have to be removed while school is still in session to prevent any delays in the demolition. At least my son's nursery school teacher—who will probably have to take early retirement under the circumstances—taught us one life lesson: *Eat up, eat up, while you can, / just don't eat your fellow man. / Or your fellow woman, nay, / let her live another day. / But if you eat them, no great loss— / Just be sure to brush and floss!*

V

Miezel

On the way to see Maria, known as Miezel, I have to drive through the valley, first down to the lowest and coldest point along the route—the road makes a sharp curve there, so it's easy to skid in the winter—then back up at the other end of the valley, then a right at the Kreuzwirt tavern, past the forest that Miezel helped plant thirty years ago—at night you can often see deer in the meadow that borders the forest, standing there as if petrified, blinded by the headlights. Today, in the sunlight, I see two figures coming toward me there: an overweight mother with her equally overweight, grown-up daughter, holding each other's hands.

The journey to see Miezel has become a very long one since I moved back to Berlin. Normally, her silhouette approaches the frosted glass panes of the door, hunched over like a crescent moon. Then Maria, known as Miezel, opens the door to me. In the time I've known her, she's grown ever thinner and more frail. Still, her hair is only gray in a few places. She wears an apron over her skirt, and slippers on her feet because of the corns. "Pain," she says, and smiles, "constant pain!"— she smiles and shakes her head as if in amazement, her feet are bony like the rest of her body, and whenever she bumps into anything, her skin immediately turns blue in that spot, since the veins are just beneath the surface.

Miezel lives in the castle where she served as a maid all her life, on the ground floor, right next to the entrance. Until just a few years ago, she was still carrying suitcases up to the third floor. She cooked, cleaned, and tended the garden for the masters of the estate. She opens the door for guests, workmen, the chimney sweep, and the postman. The bricklayer and the gardener take their lunch break in her kitchen. Miezel drinks raspberry syrup mixed with tap water, she cooks her food on an iron stove, and any leftover provisions that aren't suitable for the compost are thrown onto the fire. Miezel has never flown in an airplane. She always used to walk the three kilometers to the village on foot, back before she started to get dizzy so often. She never learned to ride a bicycle, and never used an escalator. When the masters aren't at home, she tends the castle, and her only companions are the dormouse, the Aesculapian snake, and the red salamander. The house where she was born is at the foot of the hill where the castle stands. Miezel can see it from her window.

One of the two rooms she's lived in for thirty years is the front parlor. She keeps fruit and cake there in a cool and shady place, the baskets and trays are laid out on a huge black table with lathe-turned legs that once belonged to someone or other who lived in these rooms before. The other room is the one where Miezel sleeps, her dresses and aprons are hung there in a shallow closet, and there's a TV, too, and an armchair, its upholstery already worn rather bare in the spots where Miezel places her hands on the armrests. She brings in the coffee pot, and I can see that a coffee pot like that holds weight.

Back when I was her neighbor, she would always carry something in her hands when she came to visit me—a head of lettuce, or two or three apples, or some mushrooms, or a plate of cakes. "A few Buchteln," she'd say, Austrian sweet rolls. The things she brought were things she'd planted, cooked, baked, or found in the woods

21

herself. Later, when she couldn't go into the woods or work in the garden anymore, or even cook or bake, she made me open-faced sandwiches. White bread with cheese or salami, with slices of egg or halved sour pickles on top. She arranged the slices of egg on the bread with her bony hands, and if I didn't manage to eat it all, I had to take the rest home with me wrapped in aluminum foil—for this evening, for tomorrow—along with a package of cookies for my child.

When I ring her doorbell today, it's a long time before the door is opened. Her caretaker must not be very familiar with the keys yet. High up in the sky, far above the big cherry tree, a hawk is circling. Inside, in her dimly lit kitchen, Miezel is seated at the table; her caretaker has set her there and pushed the chair close to the table so that she can hold herself upright. Miezel sits there, but she's so weak that she can't even manage to open her eyes. I look out her window. Through the bare trees, I can see as far as the house where her mother was a maid and her father was a servant. Miezel sits there motionless. Which means that when I leave, I can only hug her from the side.

VI

Junk

Of course it's nice when the eye can be at peace, when it doesn't get tangled up in knickknacks, when the drawers open silently and then close again as if by magic. It's nice to have bare tables where no dust falls, only light. It's nice when everything is made of glass and you can see through everything, because nothing else is there. Emptiness is nice. Who doesn't like to make a purchase when the salesman places a single pair of trousers on a frosted glass counter that's lit from below? Then those trousers are the last thing on earth that casts a shadow, and the counter with its bluish shimmer turns out to be an altar that leads from Berlin to Vienna, and from Vienna to Tokyo, and from Tokyo to New York, and from New York perhaps to heaven or hell, gradually narrowing as it disappears from view.

The words "German East Africa" are still legible on my battered, dusty globe. The jug with the polka dots was my great-grandmother's milk jug, my great-grand-mother mastered the art of peeling a potato in a single strip. During the war, my grandmother made that teddy bear for my mother out of a gray army blanket. My uncle kept matches with colorful sulfur heads in that little brass box for me to play with—you couldn't get them anywhere else in the East. The postal scale on my desk belonged to a friend who passed away; when I stand up on my desk to pull down the blinds, it sways gently up and down. All year round, an ancient record player sits under the piano, waiting for Christmas, because it's only at Christmas that we put the discs on the turntable and crank it up: first "Silent Night, Holy Night," and then, when it gets late, "La donna è mobile."

The Rhinelanders, Bavarians, and Swabians I meet here in Berlin tell me they prefer the Japanese style, they say they love that emptiness. No Persian apartments, please, they say, meaning the Persian carpets they inherited. Is it really just because German East Africa doesn't exist anymore? Or did Rhenish, Bavarian, and Swabian great-grandmothers lack the skill to peel potatoes in a single strip, did Rhenish, Bavarian, and Swabian uncles neglect to keep colorful matches around for the length of an entire childhood, do friends in other German states have eternal life? Maybe the Rhinelanders, Bavarians, and Swabians are simply too far away from home. Maybe the brothers and sisters they left behind have taken their place in dusty lairs in Rhineland, Swabia, or Bavaria that are full of junk, just like mine, because Berlin is my home.

But no, Berliners like the Japanese style, too, I can see that clearly: Sunday after Sunday, there's a flea market outside my window, the flea market is full, full of junk, and full of people who want to look at the junk but don't want to own it. People stroll around and leaf through strangers' photo albums, weigh the keys of long-demolished houses in their hands, smell freshly starched cloths that once belonged to someone else's grandmother: *If you're feeling tired and weary, a cool bath will help you, dearie!* As they grew up, they slowly raised their heads above the legacies of their own families, grandmother's scraps of wool and fabric slipped off of them and into the donation pile, stacks of plates and cups from the postwar period were pushed aside and smashed, they crumpled the mountain of paper—father's letters, mother's rental contracts, their own notes from their school days—under their feet, flailing for air with both arms as if they were drowning. After that, they're free to wander around the flea market, and they might buy an orange egg cup to give someone as a present. Maybe even someone else's diary in shorthand that they can't read, and don't need to. There's so much to inherit these days, so many memories, it's just too much to bear. We've been at peace for so long here that everything we have is cheap, but emptiness will soon be priceless.

VII

Cheese and Socks

The other day I bought some cheese, a particularly expensive piece of cheese, I cut myself a slice while I was standing in front of the refrigerator, and it tasted very good. That same evening, the piece of cheese was nowhere to be found—not in the refrigerator, or in any of the cabinets, or on the table, or in the freezer, or even in the toolbox, in the washing machine, in the linen closet, or on the balcony. Not in the oven, either. In fact, it had really and truly disappeared, and it stayed that way, too, it had disappeared so thoroughly that it didn't even start to stink after a while from any corner that I might have forgotten about while searching for my piece of cheese. I ask my mother, who knows her way around my house: Have you by any chance seen the cheese? She says no. I say: Did you by any chance throw it away? My mother says no.

The same thing happened to my son with the little book we kept in the bathroom to read aloud from during his longer visits: *How to Survive Situations You'll Probably Never Get Into*. It included instructions on how to fend off a crocodile, a shark, and a cougar, how to climb from a speeding motorcycle into a moving car, what to do if your parachute doesn't open, and so forth. We spent a lot of time studying that little book, so much time that I got quite tired of the page with the shark and preferred to roll down the windows while driving across a frozen lake to balance the water pressure in case of sinking—then it would be a piece of cake to get out of the car at the bottom of the lake. But suddenly that little book has disappeared. It isn't on the bookshelf, it isn't mixed in with the waste paper, it hasn't slipped behind the radiator or into the basket with the dirty laundry. I ask my mother: Have you by any chance seen our little yellow book? She says no.

Third, a single sock disappears, half of my favorite pair, but that's not at all unusual. I've heard that in probability theory there's a law concerning this very phenomenon (the Greek word for "appearance"): the law of disappearing socks. And this brings me to my hope. My hope that the disappearance of things in one place necessarily results in their appearance in another place, that there may be a world in which my sock, filled with that expensive piece of cheese, plunges from a very high bridge and survives the fall.

VIII

Safe Conduct

When I first moved in, the parklike inner courtyard of my apartment building could be entered or exited from three different points of the compass, via convoluted paths through patches of brush and between trees and flowers. Children played in this courtyard—all afternoon long they chased each other, squealed, shouted, and jumped around—foreign children who ran around in knee socks even in the winter, and who carried each other on their arms. When summer came, whole families gathered to grill in the courtyard late into the night. I could roll my bicycle right out of the storage room at ground level and leave the courtyard through one of those three passages, in whichever direction I wanted. After all, the Wall had fallen, thank God.

Shortly after I moved in, the doors that led directly from the storage room to the courtyard were permanently closed; we were told that the owner of the adjacent building did not wish to grant us right of way, and in fact she put in new flower beds all around our storage room and planted thorny shrubs. (Right of way?) Now I had to haul my bicycle upstairs and downstairs, through the hallway of the building, when I went outside. But I could still cross the courtyard, depending on how much of a hurry I was in and which direction I was headed. After all, the Wall had fallen, thank God.

By now, the apartment house where the foreign children used to live has been renovated. The neighborhood is now a "good neighborhood." The children are gone. (Right of residence?) That passage to the courtyard has been closed; outside the building, a doorbell nameplate with gold buttons has been installed. But at least I can still get to Bernauer Strasse, where the Wall once stood, by taking the same shortcut across the courtyard. Thank God.

A short time later, this second passage is also closed. I climb over the fence twice, but then I give up. The third and final entrance to the courtyard, right next to my building, can't be closed off, but that isn't even necessary anymore. That's the gate that people use to enter the courtyard, throw their trash into the bin, and then leave again. There are no cookouts anymore. (Right of sausage?) Recently, behind the garbage bins, not far from the path that's slowly becoming overgrown because it no longer leads anywhere, I found a wooden pallet lying in the brush. To someone who's spent time in cities, it looked unmistakably like the sort of spot a person prepares as a place to sleep.

IX

Friend

Now I'm going to make you disappear in this text. It's as simple as that. In you go. But why, my friend asks, that's what I'm asking you, I say, what's this all about, she asks, yes, I say, that's what I'd like to know, too. In you go, I say, then shut the lid, then everything is calm and quiet. Calm and quiet sometimes occur in friendships, and there are different kinds: calm after the storm, calm before the storm, or simply calm. This last sort of calm has something to do with the disappearance of the friendship, that much is certain; perhaps this calm isn't calm at all, but silence, and perhaps this silence itself is the cause of the silence, in which case the disappearance would be something circular.

When I'm riding my bike, little insects sometimes fly into my mouth or up my nose. And before I know it, they're in my throat, and my throat gulps them down, and there's nothing I can do but try after the fact to think of the insects as food, so that it doesn't bother me that they've ended up inside me. In the case of one of those little flies or mosquitoes, you could certainly say that it disappeared into my mouth or nose, but really it's still there, just out of sight. Whenever a little mosquito or fly disappears into my mouth and my throat gulps it down against my will, I ask myself whether just slipping out of sight is enough in itself to count as disappearance, or whether a more thorough dissolution is required.

The other question that inevitably occurs to me each time something disappears is whether anything was there to begin with—and if so, what. In the case of a friendship, for example, which is invisible from the start, it may be that the bond whose disappearance I mourn was only an appearance anyway, that in essence there were just two lonely sets of the most eclectic odds and ends that intersected for a while and are now drifting apart again.

The most encouraging reading would be that the more thoroughly a friendship disappears, the more securely it is preserved. That silence takes up just as much space and connects us just as firmly to one another as all the walks, conversations, shopping trips, afternoons spent at playgrounds, glasses of wine, and cups of coffee put together. That the answers that were not given remain faithful to me, through their absence, for all eternity. That although the disappearance has entered my body against my will, in retrospect it can be seen as nourishment, at least until I have had my fill.

X

Stoves and Coal

Never tear out one of those tiled heating stoves, a man once told me. He'd been drafted at the age of seventeen as an antiaircraft auxiliary and he'd ended up as a prisoner of war in Poland. Gas heating is well and good, but always keep at least one tiled stove in your apartment, even if it's usually just standing there cold—you should never tear it out regardless, because you never know what's going to happen. You always have to be ready to provide your own heat, he told me. Under any circumstances. Any circumstances at all, like a pretty serious war, for example. The kind of war where you lose electricity, and water, and of course you lose your central heating, too. A pretty serious war: First you would feel a tremor, and then, before you knew it, the glass windows on all the modern buildings would start raining down in tremendous showers of glass, and all of the offices would be left standing there wide open to the air, whether it was summer or fall or winter.

When I pass by the coal shop around the corner from my apartment, I see tattered 50-kilogram sacks with Czech coal almost bursting out of them. The sacks are piled up on top of each other several meters high, and next to them are equally high piles of coal briquets from Lausitz, so much black in the narrow space between two buildings that were spared by the war. When he doesn't have anything to pile up or to deliver, the coal handler stands on the sidewalk in front of the driveway, his face dusted with black, looking at the graphic designers, the marketing specialists, and the personal assistants as they hurry past on the way from their apartments with central heating to their offices with central heating. He stands there regardless of the weather, and some of the people say hello to him even though they never buy anything from him, and he returns their greetings. The briquets are from Schwarze Pumpe, he says, down at the southern end of Brandenburg, almost in Saxony. The Black Pump Combine: *Pick up your pen, coal miner*, I think, and I'm amazed that anything at all is still being produced in Schwarze Pumpe. That socialist name itself has been the butt of jokes for years, at least in this neighborhood, and now it's even the name of a café. It's cheaper from the chute, even Rekord brand, the man from the coal shop says. From the chute? My son looks down from his bicycle at the granite slabs of the sidewalk, notices the black sludge, and asks: What's that? Rain plus coal, I say. Coal? The coal man waits there for his customers, even in the rain, while the black dust slowly transforms into greasepaint that drips down his face, and it may not be long before waiting is the only job he has.

XI

Middle of Nowhere

There's an Isle of the Blessed somewhere in eastern Germany where a Ferris wheel rises up above fields of rapeseed, bran, and oats, where a boat swings, where the pop hits of the Sixties echo across the grounds, *merci, merci, merci*, where the llama grazes alongside the cow, *for the hours, chérie, chérie, chérie*, where the fox from the petting zoo plays with the boss's pug, where a cup of coffee costs fifty cents, including powdered creamer and sugar cubes from the family-size pack. Once you've entered this paradise (1 child + 1 adult = 12 euros), all the rides are free, even the bumper cars, for as long as you want. The only things that cost extra are shooting and throwing games.

The squirrel has been here since it fell out of its nest, the fox cub since it was found in a cottage garden without its mother, the monkeys are lab animals that served out their time, the goat was supposed to be put down because it was born with a cleft lip. The boss and his wife used to be travelers, but now they've made their home far away from the big cities once and for all, catapulting themselves out of their itinerant existence and settling down in the middle of nowhere, where the rent is affordable. The man from the homeless shelter who sometimes helps out here sleeps on a cot in the ticket booth when it's been a long night. He trained as a butcher. *I left my knife set with my mama.* Siblings? *My one brother, he fell in the war, the other's in Australia, I'm the only one that's left here.* Not a word about his father. And his mother? *She up and moved. One day I come back home and there wasn't nobody there no more.* And children? *Yeah, a little girl. She's gotta be ten by now.* The last time he saw her was four years ago. And since then? *She's livin' with my mama now.* And his mother? Oh, right. No registered address? *Course not.* And what if his own daughter were to show up suddenly one day, standing in line to drive the bumper cars? *Maybe we'll get the chance someday—that'd really be something.* Would you recognize her? *Yeah, I'd recognize her for sure. For sure. But the little one, she probably wouldn't recognize me no more, you know, I had a beard back then.* And your mother? *She'd always recognize me.*

The man sounds a long, wailing siren to signal the start of every round in the bumper cars, sometimes he even rides along when there's only one child there—that way the child has someone to bump into, *it wouldn't be no fun otherwise.* And if we want to ride the Ferris wheel when there's no one else around, he sits in a gondola on the other side as a counterweight, *so it don't rock too much.* When we're at the top, my son looks out over the fields and says: Wow, what a big wide world!

XII

Stolen Goods

The border opens, and people from the West bend down
from the tailgates of their trucks and give presents to
their poor sisters and brothers from the East: Christmas
is coming, and they're giving wrapping paper away for
free in the joy of reunification. But now here they come,
the evil sisters from the East, the well-educated girls who
took piano lessons at home, who know Faust's final
monologue by heart, and they stuff the West into their
pockets, they slip sunglasses from Schlecker into
their sleeves and music cassettes between the buttons
of their jackets, they tie sweaters they haven't paid for
around their waists and even walk around the store with
them on, while these things that don't belong to them
slowly absorb the heat of their bodies. Well, that's just
outrageous, these young ladies don't know what grati-
tude is (clearly they were completely ruined by the

47

Russians), they come along and just toss cheese, sausage, and coffee, even champagne bottles and chocolate, into their shopping bags, maybe they pay for the three rolls at the top, but then they stroll out of the shopping hall, which is called a supermarket nowadays, with all those other, stolen things bouncing around underneath, and those girls don't even blush. At home they practice drawing in perspective, but on the Ku'damm they put on expensive fur hats and then leave the store with alabaster faces. These same girls used to have to line up at dawn to get hold of even one copy of *The Aesthetics of Resistance* by Peter Weiss—and now that they can buy any book they want, they start stealing! The factories in the East are so dilapidated that those people can be happy if someone buys them for 1 mark: If you want to be able to afford expensive underwear, you have to work first, work until you turn old and gray, until you turn black if you have to, don't just stuff a bra down the front of your pants until you have a belly, nothing is free anymore, Christmas is over, but they don't listen, those brash young things, they drive out of the hardware store on riding lawn mowers, right past the salesman, and even give him a friendly nod, if we're not careful, they'll rob the West blind. Anno 1990.

XIII

Men

For a few weeks, there was a strong smell of cats emanating from the middle apartment on the third floor, then it grew into a stench, the windows in the hallway were left wide open during the day and even at night, and finally the animal welfare agency, acting on a tip from some neighbors, broke down the door and freed three cats that had gone mad—two more already had their insanity behind them, they were dead. On occasions like that, the animal welfare men wear helmets made of metal mesh, as if they were dressed for fencing, because the abandoned animals in their rage make no distinction between one person and another. The cats' owner, it was said, had probably simply forgotten about his animals.

In Wagner's Ring cycle, the forgetful hero Siegfried, wrapped in his airy invisibility cloak, travels swiftly from marriage to marriage; today he would probably be called a marriage swindler. A man is already thundering down the stairs, fleeing across the courtyard, when a woman shouts after him: "Get lost!"—as if these words, of all things, could persuade her beloved to stay. The fact that disappearing from one place means appearing in another can hardly be shown more beautifully than in the film *The Man Who Walked Through the Wall*, in which the tax official Buchsbaum (Heinz Rühmann) discovers one day that he is able to pass in and out of closed rooms, to move through walls as if through water. In essence, he disappears from his life as a third-tier tax official and reappears as a supernatural being. Rarely has the change of circumstances, or the change of state that necessarily accompanies the disappearance and reappearance of both people and things, gone more smoothly.

An acquaintance of mine had a child who was only three months old when her husband told her he was leaving. Then he left. Thirteen years later, he came back and befriended his daughter. Another friend had phases like that in her life, too, sometimes the moon was in its first quarter, sometimes it was full, sometimes it wasn't visible at all. The father of her child had actually acknowledged his son in advance, but he never made an appearance after the birth. When the child was one and a half, the father unexpectedly showed up at the door. For a few months he played with his son, went on outings, and even bought a Christmas tree. Then he disappeared as suddenly as he had come, and he has not been seen again; the child is seven now. In any case, disappearance is surely no less powerful than love, but it remains astonishing that thin air can sometimes have just as much weight as something that is really there.

XIV

Disassembly

We are only guests on earth, we've known that for a long time, but even before we vacate the premises altogether, we are guests time and again, as if for a trial run: in other people's apartments, summer houses, hotels. Before we vacate the premises altogether and all our baggage inevitably falls away, we have the opportunity to transport our earthly belongings to this place or that, as we please. At some point, when the time is up, a woman may come, or a man, or an owner, or a landlord, and tell us to leave. It's also possible for us to leave before we're asked to. Or to leave reluctantly, and belatedly. Finally, it's possible for us to be gone before anyone has even noticed that we were there to begin with, so that our disappearance goes entirely unnoticed. But wherever we stay, for however short or long a time, we always, at a minimum, open a door, go inside, breathe, perhaps sit on a chair, eat from plates, drink from glasses, sleep in beds, we may stock up on essentials, play games, browse through books, move the rug a bit when we go out, turn the key only once when we lock up instead of twice as the owner of the house usually does. We bring some things with us, we handle others, move them just a bit, or our smell clings to them, but in any case, when we disappear, our things are supposed to disappear as well, the mark we've made is supposed to be taken back and disappear along with us, then we have to drag all our belongings from the apartments, the houses, the rooms that we leave, the way an octopus drags its tentacles from an undersea cave.

And that's why this weekend I'm standing on a teetering platform in the branches of an oak tree, pounding on the boards of a tree house with a hammer to pry them loose, that's why I'm using a pipe wrench to unscrew the hammock hooks from tree trunks full of resin, the pipe wrench breaks and it all blows up in my face, that's why I'm deflating balls, folding chairs and tables, wrapping plates and glasses in newspaper, that's why I'm stuffing jackets and sweaters into suitcases, rubber boots and ice skates into a big bag, that's why I'm even digging up my peony at the very last minute. When you leave a hotel, you often see the doors of the rooms that have already been vacated standing open, revealing rumpled sheets, empty bottles, crumpled paper, cigarette butts and ashes. Now the rented place where we spent four summers doesn't look much different than those abandoned hotel rooms. As I'm driving away, I can barely fit into the car because so many things have grown attached to me and have to disappear with me when I leave.

XV

The Simple Life

The great advantage of an outhouse is that you never have to flush it and it doesn't freeze in the winter. Do you know how to pump it out? Well, my father used to shovel bark mulch over it, then it decomposes. Why don't you install a chemical toilet? Don't you have a pit, does it leach out, or not? It's all natural. I'd rather dig a hole in the bushes. But if you put bark mulch over it, I'm telling you, it doesn't even stink. All right, then. It's so dark right now. Here, take the flashlight with you. But something's going to jump up at me from down below. Nonsense, there's nothing living down there. You never know.

When the sun shines on the chimney, my great-grandmother used to say, the warm air somehow presses down on the fire, so it always takes longer for it to burn.

There's some kind of lever here, too, but I don't know what it does. It looks like it's rusted through. Well, I'm certainly not going to stand in this kitchen in the summer, when it's over eighty degrees, and spend two hours tending the fire just to cook potatoes. After all, you can get a hot plate with one or two burners at any home improvement store. They're not expensive, either. Food just tastes better when it's cooked on a real fire. Much better. I agree. Nonsense, heat is heat. Now my hands are all black. Where's your bathroom?

Here, there's a tap on the wall. I see. It doesn't make any difference whether you wash your hands over a sink or a bucket. Why is the water in the bucket so black? Because I poured the coffee grounds into it earlier. I can only brush my teeth with hot water. There's hot water in the pot on the stove. That's how my grandma used to do it, too! There were always three pots! And the soap suds and toothpaste? We pour them out. Where? Into the bushes. That's bad for the environment. Oh, come on.

Who's doing the dishes? Here, we'll use these two bowls. One has dish soap in it, the other one's for rinsing. I should use the hot water from the pots? Exactly. And where do I put the dishes to dry? I'll dry them right away, otherwise the utensils get rusty and stained, it's the old iron stuff from Solingen. I see. These are the best knives, you can sharpen them again and again. Ah. Where are we going to sleep anyway? Upstairs, I'll put the ladder up in a minute. And if you hear anything, it's just the martens. Can I take the flashlight with me? There are electric lights upstairs. Really? Fantastic.

XVI

Warsaw Ghetto

In the rear courtyards of the roughly two apartment buildings that remain from the Warsaw ghetto, the Catholic residents have installed glass cases for the Virgin Mary. All around the Virgin, the stench of food, beer, and fabric softener wafts from the open windows, the crumbling corners of the walls reek of cats and piss, and a cool, musty smell drifts out the open cellar doors. The Virgin can't wipe the dust off the glass that obscures my view of her. A child comes galloping diagonally across the courtyard, then disappears down a well-worn staircase into the darkness of one building that intersects the other at a right angle, a woman totters out of the entryway, a television is on. The roughly two apartment buildings that remain from the Warsaw ghetto are reinforced with iron beams that span the courtyard, there are nets and boards to catch any falling stones, balconies without floors jut out from the facade, and the plaster is long gone. These roughly two apartment buildings with their bare brick walls have been standing like this for over sixty years, but at some point they're bound to collapse.

On the spot where the smaller part of the ghetto stood over sixty years ago, there is now a nine-story hotel, that's where I'm staying. Across from my window, three glass elevators go up and down inside a glass tube. On the spot where the Aryans pried the Aryan cobblestones from the street to throw them over the three-meter-high wall at the Jews, the holes have been filled in with asphalt, and all that remains today of the Aryan streetcar that once passed beneath the Jewish bridge are a few last pieces of track. Many of the new houses that were built on the site of the ghetto after the war were constructed on the rubble and foundations of the old houses that the Germans had burned to the ground, which is probably why there's often a small slope to the right and left of the sidewalk, overgrown with grass and bushes, and the buildings themselves sit a bit higher. At Milastrasse 18, where the last fighters of the ghetto uprising took their own lives, geraniums grow on the balcony, the curtains are bleached bright white, and birds chirp from a quince tree. On the spot where the historian Emanuel

Ringelblum climbed out of the sewers to hide on the Aryan side, there's a beautiful park with large chestnut trees. The only large trees in Warsaw are outside of the area where the ghetto once stood. And in the Jewish cemetery. There, a woman is pushing a baby carriage in front of her, and when I turn to look at the child as I pass by, the carriage holds nothing but a crumpled white woolen blanket.

XVII

Courtesy

I've never been one of those women who think it's dis-
respectful for some gentleman to help them into their
coats. I like to be helped into my coat, and there have
even been times in my life when I was used to it. Sometimes, very rarely, I still experience that brief confusion
when I think, does he want to, and he thinks, does she
know, and he and I pull on the coat and twist and turn
this way and that and turn toward each other and away
from each other and don't know quite what to do. Con-
fusions of that sort have been increasing lately.

Can I still take it for granted today that a gentleman
will hold the door open for me, or that a lady will thank
me if I hold the door for her? That it's not my fault if
someone pushes me? Do mothers with baby carriages
stand at the foot or the head of the stairs late into the

night, waiting for help? If a seventeen-year-old sales clerk addresses me informally, does that mean I'm forever young? Would you please help me lift this table (solid birch) into the car? I would prefer not to, replies the Bartleby of today, a man in the prime of his life; then he gets into his car and drives past me, leaving me standing next to the solid birch table in the parking lot. There's a hair clip on the ground, is that your daughter's? Nope, it ain't. Is it this lack of dialog that leads, at other times, to so much screaming? Is that why, when my child accidentally brushes against a man with his bike, the man starts screaming at us so loudly that people all around the square take note, some cautiously approach, and others observe what's happening to us from behind the bushes? Or when a friend takes her dog out for a walk and he tries to sniff a fellow dog, the other dog's owner starts screaming and pulls his pet away by the leash?

When I was a child, there were always a few old women in line at the bakery who'd lived through the war and knew how hard it is to survive. They pushed their way to the front, they never looked right or left, they just kept their eyes on the bread and looked out for themselves. Today there are young women who know how difficult it is to survive in peacetime; they push their way to the front, they never look right or left, but sometimes, very rarely, when they realize their mistake, they apologize, and because the German word "Entschuldigung" is so rarely used that they might not even know it anymore, they say: "Sorry."

XVIII

Houses

Well, these days they're gonna do it all with excavators. Wrecking balls, that's old-fashioned stuff. They're gonna do the demolition step by step, sort it out, first they take the wood, the carpet, the pipes, haul all that old junk out of there and throw it in the dumpster. But the glass'll just get smashed up right on site, they can leave that in the house, it's made of minerals just like all the other stuff. Say a two-story house? For that kinda job I'd use a crawler excavator. One with jaws or a grapple. That way you just take the house apart piece by piece from top to bottom and drop it right into the truck or the dumpster. Start with the timber from the roof and then the masonry, of course you're workin' top to bottom. You get the roof beams with the sorting grapple, it's got kind of a groove where the plaster can fall through, then you just keep going with a grapple or a shovel, that one's got an open top for loading your materials or tearing out your foundations. Implosion? For a single-family house? Well, you might get that approved if it's a detached unit, but that's like bringing a gun to a knife fight. Besides, it's way too much work, it's not like you just drop your charge in from the top, that's gonna take a lot of manual labor. First you gotta drill. For a house like that I'd say about 200 holes. And in every single one of those holes you put your blasting dynamite. Right, blasting dynamite. But for a house like that I'd use an excavator with hydraulic cylinders. These days you might blow up a smokestack—something where you can't get at it from above. Of course they didn't have big cranes after the war, so they even blew up the tenement buildings that were right there in the gaps between the other houses, between the fire walls, they were real pros back then, like my dad. Oh sure, they used wrecking balls back then too, they called that a bomb, a cable excavator with a bomb. Destruction from below, that way the whole house just collapses, top to bottom. Oh well. What's gone is gone—won't see that again. What's a house like that weigh? You mean the tonnage? Well, if you divide the cubic meters by 0.25, that'll give you more or less the compacted mass. And then you multiply that by 2.2, on account of the density. You know water has a density of 1, and a brick sinks in water, it's denser, so for demo on a brick house you've got a density of 2.2. That puts us at right about 500 tons. But what you're gonna load onto the truck isn't compacted mass, it's more loosely packed, so there you're not gonna multiply it by 2.2, you're gonna take 1.3. Right. So you can put 18 cubic meters on a tractor trailer, and your tractor trailer's gonna make two or three round trips a day, for a house like that you're gonna need about seventeen round trips. Right, to one of the construction dumps outside the city. One of these days they're all gonna be shut down and covered over, then they'll just go back to being landscape.

XIX

Mothers

My four-year-old son is standing at the airport, he's not crying. He isn't screaming either, he's not stamping his feet or calling me names. He's just standing there, keeping very quiet. The evening before my departure, he made me a triptych of pieces of paper with his name on them, then in the morning he took a slimy heart, actually a gruesome toy, laid it on a piece of paper, and traced its outline with a red ballpoint pen. But because the slimy heart looked like a real heart, which means the outline looked like a sofa cushion, he added a few normal hearts, the kind you usually see in pictures, to make sure I'd understand. As we were leaving the apartment, he quickly stuck one of his pirate stickers on my arm to bring me luck. And now he's standing there, and he's not crying.

"Ten days is a long time for a child," everyone says, but everyone also knows that it's much more dangerous to drive from Berlin to Munich by car than to get on an airplane. Nevertheless, I made my last will and testament three years ago, before I got on an airplane without my child for the first time. The little one doesn't know how dangerous it is to drive from Berlin to Munich, nor does he know that because he's a child, the ten days will seem very long to him, and he certainly doesn't know what a last will and testament is, but he knows that he has to make this farewell good enough that it could last forever if need be—he sees that in my departure, which is just as real as a departure that lasts forever. I'm standing there with a pirate sticker on my arm, next to my big suitcase, close to the check-in counter, and I'm not crying, either.

It's 379 miles to St. John and 671 to Corner Brook, we have 2716 miles behind us and 1413 ahead of us. We're flying through the air at 905 kilometers per hour, flying with the sun, as they say, or you could just as well say that we're hovering in the air at a speed of 905 kilometers per hour, just letting the earth spin down below us until the city we're heading for eventually arrives. When I look out the window, I see nothing but water, and the waves are tiny white streaks that neither roll nor break nor move in any other way. Apparently I'm too far away to recognize anything on earth now. The ocean looks like stone from so high up, and the stewardesses, I realize now, are much older than any stewardesses I've ever seen before. Stern ladies who might slap you on the wrist if you spill your coffee. Will I perhaps have to stay here forever, too, with the pirate sticker on my arm, in this no-man's-land high up in the air, far above the frozen water, will I perhaps have to grow old in flight here, too, as old as the stewardesses, and older and older still?

XX

Drip Catchers

The carpet hangers disappeared from the rear courtyards when wall-to-wall carpeting and vacuum cleaners were introduced—after the Persian carpets had been bombed away, when there was no money to buy new ones, and the men who used to carry the rolled-up carpets down the stairs for cleaning had been killed in the war.

The shop where I used to take my tights to be mended when they had a run in them, back when I was a little girl—a shop called Run Express—disappeared when the Wall came down and the West was able to sell its cheap tights in the East.

The drip catchers that graced the spouts of the large coffee pots that used to sit on the table at every German family reunion—those drip catchers disappeared when the children born during the last days of the war finally rebelled against their parents and stopped planning family reunions, preferring instead to travel to Italy and bring back espresso makers from there.

Things disappear when they are deprived of their means of existence, as if they, too, have a hunger that must be satisfied. And even if the reasons for their disappearance are infinitely far removed from the things themselves—as far removed, say, as the crimes of the German Wehrmacht are from German coffee, which is always far too weak, served in those pear-shaped pots it always tried to trickle down until it was held in check by the drip catcher, a little roll of foam rubber on an elastic band decorated with a butterfly, a doll, or a pearl perched atop the lid of the pot, a little thing that protected white tablecloths in Germany from coffee stains until the mid-1970s—even then, no matter how far removed the thing itself might be from the fashion, the invention, or the revolution that leads to its disappearance, that disappearance creates a bond that could not be tighter. For example, the Berlin painter Heinrich Zille once said that you could kill a person with an apartment just as easily as with an ax.

So the little roll of foam rubber and its elastic bridle end up in the trash, which means that now Germans are rich enough to afford vacations in Italy again and to bring back espresso makers in their luggage when they return. Just as each thing, no matter how simple, contains within it all the knowledge of its time, just as everything you can't touch is contained in a spool of darning thread, for example; in the same way, whenever a thing disappears from everyday life, much more has disappeared than the thing itself—the way of thinking that goes with it has disappeared, and the way of feeling, the sense of what's appropriate and what's not, what you can afford and what's beyond your means. We don't have darning thread anymore! Really, why? People shouldn't darn their tights, they should buy new ones!

XXI

Words

Today, at long last, the fair maiden dons her finest robe, gathers up her diamond jewelry, emerges from her chamber, and, thus arrayed, graces the humble alley with her presence (passing by Dr. Müller's ENT practice as she descends the staircase). No sooner does she alight there than the bold knight she has been pining for arrives on the most spirited of steeds (crossing the intersection of Schwedter and Kastanienallee). Make haste, make haste, thou gallant man! The fair maiden says to herself: What a delight he is to behold, I can ne'er avert my eyes from him, oh, if only he would deign to hear me! But soft, now doth he cast the pure light of his eyes upon me. (The bell of the elementary school rings to announce the first recess.) The rider pulls at the reins of his horse, he stammers, he falters, his blood is boiling, the most beauteous of maidens chastely lowers her eyes to her bodice, he springs from his horse, leads the noble animal aside by the reins (bicycles may not be parked in the foyer), then approaches his lady, bows his head, and greets her, she demurs, then he grows bolder and presses her ardently to his heart before she knows what is happening to her. She trembles. She says to herself: Yes, by God, the long-awaited day has come at last, when the most valiant of all knights, the most virtuous of all youths, will lead me home. (Let's go up to your place and order a pizza, or do you want falafel?) Forthwith, he says, for I hunger, I thirst, wouldst thou guide me to the secret portal? She bids him follow her (first into the courtyard, she wants to throw the garbage into the dumpster), but no sooner have they escaped the watchful eyes of the vulgar rabble than he defames her as a filthy whore, rips the jewels from her neck, cast off your trinkets, he says, and takes them to himself. (What, are you crazy?) Alas, but the foolhardy young man grows ever more impetuous and vehement. The fair maiden says to herself: All too late have I discerned that this man, whom I took for a paragon of his sex, is a godless wretch, a depraved lecher, a villainous rascal! What a disgrace! (Hey, what's wrong with you?) Begone from me, false devil, she cries, seizing the wicked man's left ear in a tangle of hair, as bitter teardrops flow from

82

his eyes. Relent, thou fool! Have mercy, fair maiden, he rejoins, lest I perish. On your knees! she cries, repent! And the hero kneels in the dirt, kneels there, and if he hasn't died, he's still kneeling there today. (But she casts his teardrops, his ardor, forsooth, the whole wicked man and his horse, and in like wise her own pleasure, her chastity, her robe, and a few other things she no longer remembers, into the trash.) Exit stage left.

XXII

Presents

It's true, at Christmas markets I'm always getting swept along with the crowd, past the same scented lamps and hand-twisted candles—whenever I want to stop to buy something, hundreds of people start whistling behind me to clear the traffic jam. It's true, the large photos I ordered for the photo calendar turn out to be small when they arrive, and a new order will take three business days to process, which means it won't get here until after Christmas Eve. It's true: My father asks me what he should get my husband, and my mother asks me what she should get my father's wife, and my husband asks me what he should get my sister, and none of them ask me what they should get my child, because they all know, and I say: Just not too many big things, because they won't fit into the nursery. In the days leading up to Christmas, I sweat in my fur coat in the copy shop,

I lug things around, I lose hats, I place orders, I measure picture frames, I browse at a lot of bookstores, I even intend to knit again, but I can't find my needles, I glue and cut, I'm often up late at night, until half past one, and all because my golden rule is: Three presents (big or small) for everyone! Abundance! Asymmetry! And fairness! Year after year, the gift exchange takes far too long, my child really should have gone to bed hours ago, I think of the difference between permutation and combination that I learned in math class, because one of the two is surely to blame for the duration of our gift-giving revelries: 7 people, each of whom gives 3 presents to each other person, doesn't just make 3 times 7, but 7 times 7 times 3. Or something like that. And if we allow at least 3 minutes to unwrap each gift, that makes 441 minutes. Or something like that. The pile of folded wrapping paper next to my mother is growing, the basket where the ribbons are collected to be reused next year will soon be overflowing, the ancient record player that we only bring out once a year, at Christmas, and crank up by hand has long since ceased to play "Silent Night, Holy Night," now it's moved on to "La donna è mobile" or the waltz from the operetta *Beloved Augustin*. Every year during the Christmas holidays, when we're completely exhausted from giving and receiving presents, fattened up from the goose, and tired from all the sleeping in, we stagger through the streets to visit friends, and our friends say: Well, we haven't given each other presents for four years now, it's much more relaxed that way. Or something like that.

XXIII

Years

At a certain point in the course of time, there is a sudden bang, and the year that has been called the present for an entire year disappears from the present and turns into the past, from one second to the next. In that second, I think of the second a year ago when the year before that year turned into the past, and I wonder what will happen in another year's time, when the span of time that has just slipped into the window of the present, the time we refer to by the number 2008, for example, falls out of that window again and into the hole in time that we call New Year's Eve. He cast his blessing on his time, as we say in German of someone who has died, and with that, he disappeared into the year in which he died, the year carries him off, takes him away; on the other hand, we could just as well say of someone else who has just been born not only that he came into the world in this or that place, but also that he came into time in this or that year, for it is no less true that he was deposited by the year of his birth.

In this second in which one number opens and another closes, I think backward and forward, as if one moment could be seen in relation to another, as long as the distance between them, measured in years, always remains the same. Backward and forward. With each recurrence, I want to believe in the ethereal web, the floating landscape of time, whose paths run between birthdays, weddings, deaths, and other anniversaries, instead of between houses. But as I wait for the moment when a church bell actually strikes twelve, as I hold a bottle of champagne at the ready, as I switch on the radio to hear the official time, as I stand on the balcony, listening like a blind woman for the moment when the noise will finally break out all around me, as I wait for that one second in which I will be connected to all other people by time, I suddenly realize again how little this second really differs from all the other seconds in a year, then the web of time suddenly looks so small, no bigger than a handkerchief, with so much darkness behind it and in front of it and next to it and above it and below it, and all the banging and screaming that flies across the time zones is suddenly nothing more than our own sound with which we seize this man-made moment, as we become aware that we are falling, and as if in a great wave that sweeps across the globe, friends and strangers sink into each other's arms for a few seconds, while those who have remained alone cry out, individually but all together, yellow, green, red, and silver lights travel around our planet, we drink and dance, and for a second we all hope that eternity might be a place where we can find a home.

XXIV

Empty Spaces

Every city has those places where the pavement is full of holes, where the bushes stink, where people toss their old clothes, where drunks smash empty bottles, styrofoam crumbles, sheet metal gets bent out of shape, dogs piss, posters get torn from their cardboard backing. Those places were especially numerous in Berlin after 1945: barren sites, often on street corners, where nothing grew, not even a kiosk. The sky above Berlin was always very wide, precisely because it had its counterpart on the earth below: the vast, open spaces left by bombs in Berlin.

About twenty-five years ago, I could look out the window of my childhood bedroom, across a playground, across sheds, across a storage yard for building materials: all the way to a bare fire wall, part of a single building that had been left standing all by itself, close to the West.

There were a good five hundred meters between me and the sunset back then, the horizon was a black line high in the sky with chimneys and antennas on top, and the roof of the building sloped down toward the street. At that distance, lit from behind, it looked like a paper cutting, and nowhere in the world did the sunset produce such towering urban paper cuttings as in Berlin.

Once, just two years ago, I caught some goats that had escaped from the animal show at the Circus Aron to graze on the strip of grass along the Wall right around the corner from where I live. Occasionally I've seen horses from a carriage company put out to pasture on that same spot, and from time to time I've picked wild-flowers right there, where the border patrol used to keep watch.

At one point in the 1950s there were plans to broaden Friedrichstrasse. That's probably why the open spaces there weren't built up again. Instead, there were foun-tains at the corner where Friedrichstrasse crossed the boulevard Unter den Linden, and flower beds.

By now the sunset panorama of my childhood has been blocked out by a high-rise that casts its shadow on the street and cuts the view to the west so short that it's no longer recognizable. By now the strip of grass along the Wall just around the corner from where I live has been partly fenced off: on one lot a pit has been excavated, clearly in preparation for a building project, at the bottom of the pit the foundation bricks of the houses that once stood there stick up out of the earth, and an advertisement on the fence promotes "explosive removal services"; another section of the horse and goat pasture has been transformed into a used car dealership, and cars, some of them battered, others not, are parked there on the gray gravel; and the third stretch of weedy ground has been home, for more than a year now, to people living in newly built apartments with large windows, the building is occupied all the way up to the sixth floor.

Friedrichstrasse was narrow until the end of the war, and now it's narrow again, it was full of shops packed close together, and now it's full of shops packed close together again. At the corner of Friedrichstrasse and Unter den Linden, on the very spot where the fountain once stood, we're now supposed to spring for luxury limousines, so that the company can earn back the rent that it pays. Before the war, sandstone buildings with columns were modern, and now sandstone buildings with columns are modern again, so it turns out that the period of empty spaces was just a pause.

I once heard that when the disorder within one system decreases, the disorder in an adjacent system necessarily increases. And since disorder can only emerge in spaces that are left open, I would be interested to know what emptiness looks like when it wanders. In any case, the residents of the Mitte district of Berlin now have to deal with the fact that everything is there, and nothing is missing. And Christian Morgenstern? Maybe Morgenstern lived in Mitte, too.

> *There used to be a picket fence*
> *with space to gaze from hence to thence.*

> *An architect who saw this sight*
> *approached it suddenly one night,*

> removed the spaces *from the fence*
> *and built of them a residence.*

> *The picket fence stood there dumbfounded*
> *with pickets wholly unsurrounded,*

> *a view so naked and obscene,*
> *the Senate had to intervene.*

> *The architect, however, flew*
> *to Afri- or Americoo.*

XXV

Splitterbrötchen

There are only two bakeries in Berlin-Mitte that still make Splitterbrötchen as I know them: a dense, almost chewy pastry dough without raisins, neither round nor square in shape, but rather jumbled up, as if the baker had stuck all the leftover scraps of dough together and baked something irregular. The taste should be sweet, but not too distinctly sweet; it should be crispy on the outside and soft on the inside; a Splitterbrötchen hardly crumbles at all, it isn't very big, and it tastes best with nothing on it but butter. However, what most bakeries nowadays call a Splitterbrötchen is a thing that looks a bit like a Danish pastry from the outside, a huge, squarish roll made of crumbly layers of puff pastry with plenty of air in between them.

And why?

Because that's how it's taught today at the training schools of the bakers' guild.

I see.

You take your dough, add fat, fold it over 3 to 5 times, depending on how you like it—that's the beauty of being a creative baker: the variations.

Yes, but I'm not interested in the variations, I'm interested in the essentials. Today's Splitterbrötchen is something fundamentally different from the Splitterbrötchen twenty years ago.

It's the same as it always was: You take your dough, add fat, fold—

It never had anything to do with fat, a Splitterbrötchen was sweet, and—

But it does taste sweet! You can fold it over 3 times or 5 times, or even once or twice for all I care, of course everyone does it diff—

No! The whole roll looked different, it wasn't layered!

Yes it was, it was always layered, otherwise it wouldn't be called a Splitterbrötchen.

It's called a Splitterbrötchen because the pieces of dough are stuck together—

No, it's called that because of the layers! At the end you make a hole with your thumb to let air in and then—

Air!?!

For the first time, it strikes me that the word *disappear* has something active at its core, that there is a perpetrator in the word who makes things that I know and cherish disappear: Dismantle, discard, disband, disparage, discredit, disembowel, disuse. And the one who has all this on his conscience has also made my Splitterbrötchen disappear, he has disappeared it, he has taken something that I knew well, something that I loved to eat, and locked it out of all the bakeries (except two in Berlin-Mitte), he has driven it out, and now he's waiting until my memory of what a Splitterbrötchen should actually taste and look like has DISsipated and DISsolved. He stands on the threshold of his office in the bakers' guild, but he's not standing there to empty his mind of all thoughts, as the bakers' apprentices once had to do to pass their journeyman's exams, instead, he's blocking the door so that my Splitterbrötchen can never come back, and as he stands there, he thinks to himself: *The wind has carried it away—Where to? No one can ever say* . . .

XXVI

Substantive Commentaries

"One of a kind, that Beethoven!" exclaims the announcer after playing the umpteenth movement of Beethoven's umpteenth symphony: "One of a kind, that Beethoven!" The announcer stands beside Beethoven and pats him on the shoulder, and Beethoven, who is half deaf, or maybe completely deaf by now, flinches beneath the blow—that's the beauty of radio, that you can see all those things. That's why I can also see how this or that orchestra, under its conductor, Mr. What's-his-name, "takes on" Tchaikovsky's Concerto No. X, charging at the concerto full force as if heading into battle, I can see the impact, which must be especially hard on the violins and double basses in the very front. Another time, this or that philharmonic orchestra played under "a dynamic Herbert von Karajan," and I see the dynamic Herbert von Karajan on the shelf, alongside the lyrical Herbert and the restrained and the poignant and probably also the one of a kind Herbert von Karajan, standing next to each other like dolls—all of them for sale. I hear and see things that couldn't be heard or seen on the radio in the past. The less knowledge is expected or demanded of the listener, the closer those listeners are invited to come: Suddenly Beethoven stands shoulder to shoulder not only with the announcer, but also with me, where I personally don't want him to be. Now it's not just Herbert von Karajan who's dynamic, the commentary is dynamic, too, the commentary that's intended to build a bridge to him, a bridge to the classical music that may soon lose its last listeners, but in reality that bridge is a wobbly pontoon, the commentary paddles after the music with the suggestible listeners in tow, instead of offering them dry land to stand on as they gaze out at this or that sea.

One last holdover from those bygone years when keeping one's distance was still regarded as a sign of good manners is the Sunday music puzzle. For forty years, the announcer has posed riddles about Hildegard Knef, the Pizzicato Polka, or Alexandre Dumas with an innocence often presumed lost, giving his listeners time to reach for a pen and paper and write down the letters they've guessed, and I can see that, just as you can see everything clearly on the radio. But by the time we're old—and it won't be very long now—we'll be able to use this or that internet search engine to identify the composer of the "Ode to Joy" immediately as that one of a kind Beethoven, and thus to solve every riddle once and for all.

XXVII

A Better World

"How often in gray hours, O glorious art, / When life ensnares me in its circle wild, / Hast thou enkindled love within my heart / And raptured me into a better world!"—these are the words to one of Schubert's songs. But I have to: Call the insurance company, go to the doctor, the car has a red emissions sticker, do you want digital cable? Sign a form for the child, book the flight to X, which hotel, have you ever played the lottery? Get passport photos, please submit the direct debit authorization in writing by mail or fax, buy plants for the balcony, take out the trash, do the laundry, load the dishwasher, pack my suitcase. WHAT ARE YOU WORKING ON AT THE MOMENT? This is the phone company, Mr. Müller speaking. Pick up a book at the bookstore, buy stamps, buy hay for the animals, someone will be picking up the key, register the child for the swim meet, take out the trash, do the laundry, load the dishwasher, pack my suitcase. Buy water. Where's my car? Where's the key to the apartment? Why won't the cassette player eject the cassette? Get a hepatitis A booster, make an appointment with the ophthalmologist, an appointment with the gynecologist, an appointment with the pediatrician. YOU MUST BE WRITING SOMETHING NEW BY NOW, RIGHT? Pack my suitcase. Which hotel? Where are my sunglasses? The bread is moldy. My car has a red emissions sticker. Take out the trash, do the laundry, load the dishwasher, pack my suitcase. Buy potting soil. Plant flowers. It's his birthday, it's her birthday, please pay the bill within 7 days, and a parking ticket, you can contest it, where's the school trip going, pick up a book, pick up photos, buy water. YOU'LL HAVE SOMETHING NEW FOR US TO READ SOON, RIGHT? Trash, laundry, dishes. Who's going to water the flowers? Get the summer clothes out of the cellar, leave the key, pack the suitcase. Which city? Forgot my cell phone charger. DO YOU KNOW WHAT YOUR NEXT BOOK WILL BE CALLED? Why doesn't the video camera show the picture when it's recording anymore? Good evening, Meier speaking, we're doing a survey. Gas up the car, a package for you, call the bank, book the babysitter for Friday, pay the bill, change the light bulb, hang up the wet towels, book the flight, sign here, please fill out the application by hand, why is my bike rattling, buy stamps, buy hay for the animals. WHEN IS YOUR NEW NOVEL COMING OUT?

My new novel, I'd say, right, right, I'm in the thick of it right now, in the new novel, head over heels, working, working on the new novel, I mean. Because what else can it mean when life's wild circle is whirling around me with its two demented circular knitting needles, when it's been whirling around me for some time now, when life's wild circle has almost completely knitted me up, what else can it mean but that the moment of rapture has in fact long since arrived, that the rapture has long since been as deep inside me as possible.

XXVIII

Cemetery Visits

My grandmother once saw a mallard duck sitting on her recently deceased husband's gravestone, looking at her. She told us that it was her husband, who had appeared to her as a male duck to let her know that he was still alive in another form, she remained firmly convinced of it, and she brought it up again every time the conversation turned to her husband, or death, or the cemetery. My mother smiled, my uncle smiled, but my grandmother kept on believing in that duck. Many Sundays I went along to the cemetery, to the spot where first my great-grandmother, then my grandmother's husband, and finally my grandmother herself were laid to rest. My grandmother knew the grave that would become her own well before she died. For decades, she covered that small plot with fir-tree boughs in the winter, planted pansies or begonias in the spring, and now and then she put fresh flowers in the green plastic vases. For decades, she was one of the many old women you always see in cemeteries, holding a watering can in her hand, tottering back and forth from the water spigot to the grave, one of the many who throw the dead pansies, roots and all, onto the compost pile, who buy flower arrangements from the florist at the entrance to the cemetery on the last Sunday before Advent, when we observe the Sunday of the Dead, one of the many who prepare the graves for winter. As a child, I was allowed to help rake the path in front of the grave, water the flowers, pull weeds, or gather leaves from the small hedge, later I carried the watering can, still later I carried two watering cans at once, especially when it was a hot summer.

These days, I can always tell that it's the Sunday of the Dead because there's no flea market in front of my house. My uncle takes me to the cemetery on the Sunday of the Dead. It would never occur to anyone in the family that I could take on the responsibility of preparing my great-grandmother's and grandmother's graves for the winter, periodically planting pansies there or digging them up, watering them in the heat of the summer. On Sundays, my son likes to go to the children's farm, which is very close to the cemetery, but when I try to show him the grave, I get lost and can't find it. Another member of our family lies in some other cemetery, in a grave that's been tended by the staff for years, and yet another is buried under a green lawn, reservations for that lawn filled up quickly, because more and more people are choosing to decompose anonymously these days. Some of us who are still among the living plan to have our ashes scattered over the Baltic Sea.

XXIX

Things

Each time I take a long trip, I lose at least one scarf or hat, sometimes even a pair of sunglasses or a watch. I've also lost a number of things when moving house: a piece of molding from an old rustic wardrobe, a few blinds, and once I even lost the typewriter I used to write my first works. Although the hotel rooms I left were small, and the apartments I left were clearly empty, the things were still missing later; somehow, somewhere, they had disappeared in the no-man's-land between departure and arrival, it happened so regularly that I began to expect it when packing my suitcase or my boxes, as if it were a sacrifice, a price I had to pay for the change in my circumstances, and in that respect, despite all the randomness, it was still appropriate. However, in the course of my everyday life, the number of things around me never decreased, but rather increased, the piles grew higher, the folders thicker, I could imagine that a fire would break out and I would tuck my diaries, letters, and photo albums under my arm and run out of the house, but fortunately no fire broke out.

Recently, a Russian woman came to visit me. She moved to Germany a year ago with four children. A piano, how lovely! she says as she enters my apartment. Books, how lovely! A few steps farther on, she points to a few of my son's drawings hanging on the wall and says: Lovely! She adds: It's lovely to have something like that. At first, I don't understand what she means; after all, she has four children herself. Well, she says, and smiles, you can't take it all with you. Sure, sure, I say. So, she says, still smiling, we made a big bonfire, we all sat around it, then we took page after page in our hands, we looked at everything again and remembered who drew this or that, how old he or she was at the time, we enjoyed it together one last time, and then we burned it all. It was a lovely bonfire, we were singing. I don't say anything now. You can't take it all with you, she repeats, and says with a smile: We left with four children and two large suitcases. That was all.

XXX

Youth

And I can't raise my arms so well anymore, she says, and her eyes survey her body as if it were something alien. She looks just the same as always, maybe a little older than she did thirty years ago, but definitely not like an old woman. You know, I'll be seventy next week, she says, speaking in a voice that sounds just the way her voice sounded thirty years ago. Next week I'm going to the Baltic Sea for a spa treatment, she says. I'm sure it will be nice. "To the Baltic Sea," she says, no differently than she might have said it to a lover thirty years ago.

Where does all the time go, I once read in the letters of a girl who had to live apart from her parents for two years in fascist Germany. A year later she was dead, killed by the Nazis. Where does all the time go?

The illnesses that begin to afflict us take us by surprise, they set our bodies in motion in different ways than we intend, slowing them down, speeding them up, disturbing their rhythm. They take us by surprise. The years leave their marks on our skin, which was still a child's skin only recently, they leave the brown marks of old age, they make small letters blur before our eyes, they take us by surprise, and because it all happens so slowly, we don't even understand when the transition took place, slowly the years carry men's youth away, one hair at a time, they gradually, very gently, crease women's skin, and we, we remain in that skin, we see with those eyes, which now perceive small letters as an illegible blur, but we don't see signs of aging in our own thoughts, and that's why we're taken by surprise when the years have slipped over us like a dress, and we think that actually, if we wanted to, we could take them off again, that's why our arms appear to grow more unfamiliar to us the older they get, to grow more distant the more they try to force us to acknowledge their closeness by confronting us with pain and impossibilities, that's why we're taken by surprise when our own exhaustion makes us faint, and when we consider the fact that death is drawing nearer to us, one friend at a time, we'd prefer to forget that our lives often last longer than our ability to grow older.

XXXI

The Author

Surely you've also heard the theory that the author is disap ...

Mind Over Matter

A Toughness Toolbox for Soccer

GameReady Books

Table of Contents